When NEIL ARMSTRONG Built a Wind Tunnel

by Mark Weakland

illustrated by Luciano Lozano

PICTURE WINDOW BOOKS

a capstone imprint

Neil Armstrong lived an amazing life. He flew fighter planes. He went faster than the speed of sound. He became America's best-known astronaut — the first person to stand on the moon.

How did Neil do so much? As a kid, he studied and worked hard. He set goals. He dreamed big.

"Some day I want to go to that moon," he said.

And one day he did.

Neil Alden Armstrong was born on August 5, 1930. He and his parents lived on the family farm in St. Marys, Ohio. Neil's grandmother delivered him into the world.

Neil was a traveler right from the start. He loved to go places, even if it was just a trip around the farm. His grandpa put him on a pony and walked him down the road and back.

"I'll help you work, Grandpa," said Neil.

Neil was a traveler, but he wasn't always a *happy* traveler. His father was an auditor. His job involved lots of driving, often over long, twisting country roads. Little Neil went along for the rides. On almost every journey, he got carsick.

"You look a bit green in the gills, son," his mother said.

But motion sickness wouldn't keep Neil from wanting to travel, whether in a car or an airplane.

Neil got his first ride in an airplane when he was 6 years old. His father was driving him to Sunday school, and along the way they passed an airfield. There sat *The Tin Goose*, an airplane with three propellers. Its pilot was giving people rides. Neil and his father got in line.

Before takeoff, Neil's father was nervous. But not Neil. He helped buckle in his dad. When the propellers started spinning, Neil grinned.

But reaching for the sky in an airplane was not enough for Neil.
At age 9, he got a small telescope. He gazed into it for hours without
saying much. His friends thought Neil was dreaming of going into space.

Later, Neil and his friends made a great discovery. A neighbor,
Jacob Zint, had a telescope too — one with an 8-inch (20-centimeter)
lens. Mr. Zint kept it in an observatory atop his garage.

"Do you think he'll let us look through it?" asked Neil.

The answer was yes. And so began a lifelong friendship between
Neil and Mr. Zint.

Neil knew that to reach the stars, he would need to work hard.
He got his first paying job at age 10. He cut grass in a cemetery.
"Nobody here complains that I'm only 10 years old!"
he said. For his summer work, he was paid 10 cents an hour.

    In winter, Neil worked at a local bakery. It was a good job for
a small, strong boy. He was the perfect person to crawl inside the
ovens and clean them.

When he wasn't working, Neil often rode his bicycle to the nearby airport. There he did odd jobs for the pilots. One day a man asked him to help clean his airplane. Neil wiped its windows and polished its silvery skin. In return, the man offered to take Neil for a ride.

After a few minutes in the air, the man nodded toward the control stick. **"Want to take it?"** he asked.

"Yes, sir!" said Neil.

And just like that, Neil was flying the plane!

Neil was a curious kid, whether he was in the air or on the ground. Scouting allowed him to explore the world around him. He learned how to build fires and tie knots. He learned how to face his fears and be part of a team. By working hard and never giving up, Neil reached Scouting's highest rank, Eagle Scout.

As a teenager, Neil saved his money. With it he paid for flying lessons. He also paid for the gadgets he liked to build.

Once, Neil and his brother built a wind tunnel in the basement. "To be an aeronautical engineer, you've got to have a wind tunnel," Neil said. Just as their mother came down the steps, Neil turned it on. The blast of air nearly knocked her over — and broke a window!

Neil wasn't just smart about building gadgets. In school, he often stumped his teachers with questions. He was smart and worked hard. As a result, his teachers pushed him quickly through the grades.

Neil could have graduated from high school at age 15! But his parents thought he was too young to graduate. So Neil waited. Besides, he did really well only in the subjects he loved, such as math and science. In English he was average. And he failed art, typing, and social studies.

In addition to being very smart, Neil was reserved. Even as a teenager, he was more quiet and serious than loud and playful. His sense of humor was clever, not silly. But now and again, he'd pull a prank.

Once, while marching in the high school band, he turned his cap around. Then he marched backward — still playing his horn. The kids thought Neil was funny. The band director, however, did not.

Despite his pranks, Neil took his flying seriously. One morning in 1946, Neil got up extra early. He ran outside, leaped onto his bike, and pedaled hard. Today was the day. He was going to earn his flying license!

Neil reached the airport in minutes. After reading the rulebook one last time, he took his written test. Then he showed his teachers everything he knew about flying a plane. Neil passed, with excellent scores. He was just 16 years old.

"Who needs a car?" he said. "I'm licensed to fly!"

Neil's flights were just beginning. After high school, he went to Indiana. He studied at Purdue University. He also joined the U.S. Navy. When the Korean War (1950–1953) began, Neil stopped his studies and became a full-time pilot. He flew 78 missions and even survived a crash landing.

When Neil returned from Korea, he finished school. He worked as a test pilot. In the X-15, he hit speeds of almost 4,000 miles (6,437 kilometers) per hour!

But even greater things still lay ahead for Neil Armstong — in places far, far beyond the clouds.

In the 1960s, Neil started a family. He also trained as an astronaut. Neil was cool under pressure. And he knew a lot about engineering. This made him the perfect person to lead the United States' first manned mission to the moon: Apollo 11.

On July 16, 1969, Michael Collins, Edwin E. "Buzz" Aldrin, and Neil Armstrong launched into space. They traveled nearly 240,000 miles (386,243 km) to the moon. It was Neil who piloted the Lunar Module to the surface. On July 20, 1969, he jumped from the module and became the first human to set foot on extraterrestrial soil. As more than 1 billion people listened, he spoke these words: **"That's one small step for man, one giant leap for mankind."** The Apollo 11 astronauts became instantly famous. In New York City, crowds lined the streets and cheered.

After his moon trip, Neil lived a quiet life. He became a college teacher. He shared his ideas about the importance of space travel. **"Earth is the cradle of the mind,"** he said. **"But one cannot live in the cradle forever."** Just like when he was a kid, Neil was dreaming big.

Neil Armstrong died at age 82 on August 25, 2012.

GLOSSARY

aeronautical—having to do with the science and practice of designing and building aircraft

Apollo—a Greek and Roman god; all U.S. space missions to the moon were named after Apollo

astronaut—a space pilot or traveler

auditor—a person who reviews money accounts

engineer—a person who uses science and math to plan, design, and build things

extraterrestrial—coming from beyond Earth

Korean War—(1950–1953) fighting between North Korea and South Korea; the United States aided South Korea

Lunar Module—the self-contained part of the larger spacecraft that landed on the moon

observatory—a structure designed to study outer space

reserved—quiet and serious

telescope—an instrument made of lenses and mirrors that is used to view distant objects

READ MORE

McReynolds, Linda. *Eight Days Gone*. Watertown, Mass.: Charlesbridge, 2012.

Rau, Dana Meachen. *Neil Armstrong*. Rookie Biographies. New York: Children's Press, an imprint of Scholastic Inc., 2014.

Yasuda, Anita. *Neil Armstrong*. Icons: History Makers. New York: AV2 by Weigl, 2014.

CRITICAL THINKING
★ QUESTIONS ★

1) Name two childhood character traits or abilities of Neil Armstrong. How did they help him reach his goal of being the first person to walk on the moon?

2) The author says Neil never forgot the lessons he learned in Scouting. In fact, Neil used what he learned, such as the lesson of "leave no trace" on the moon. What other lessons might Neil have learned as a child and then used on the moon? Use evidence in the text to support your answer.

3) Make a timeline of Neil Armstrong's life, from the time he was born to the time he returned from the moon.

INTERNET SITES

Use FactHound to find Internet sites related to this book:

Visit *www.facthound.com*

Just type in 9781515815754 and go.

Super-cool stuff! Check out projects, games, and lots more at
www.capstonekids.com

OTHER TITLES IN
★ THIS SERIES ★

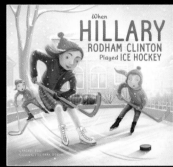
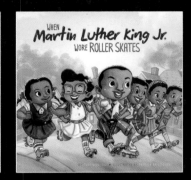

INDEX

Special thanks to our adviser for his advice and expertise:

Timothy N. Thurber, Professor of History
Virginia Commonwealth University, Richmond, Virginia

Editor: Jill Kalz
Designer: Russell Griesmer
  Creative Director: Nathan Gassman
Production Specialist: Katy LaVigne
The illustrations in this book were created digitally.

Editor's Note: Direct quotations in the main text are indicated by **bold** words.
Direct quotations are found on the following pages:
Page 2, line 6: Wagener, Leon. *One Giant Leap: Neil Armstrong's Stellar American Journey*. New York: Forge, 2004, p. 33.
Page 7, line 5: Ibid, p. 45.
Page 12, line 3: Barbree, Jay. *Neil Armstrong: A Life of Flight*. New York: Thomas Dunne Books/St. Martin's Press, 2014, p. 183.
Page 15, line 7: Ibid, p. 37.
Page 28, line 8: Wilford, John N. "Men Walk on the Moon," *New York Times*. 21 July 1969. 22 April 2017.
http://www.nytimes.com/learning/general/onthisday/big/0720.html
Page 28, lines 11–12: Barbree, Jay. *Neil Armstrong: A Life of Flight*. New York: Thomas Dunne Books/St. Martin's Press, 2014, p. 341.

Picture Window Books are published by Capstone, 1710 Roe Crest Drive, North Mankato, Minnesota 56003
www.mycapstone.com

Library of Congress Cataloging-in-Publication Data
Names: Weakland, Mark, author. | Lozano, Luciano, 1969– illustrator.
Title: When Neil Armstrong built a wind tunnel / by Mark Weakland ; illustrated by Luciano Lozano.
Description: North Mankato, Minnesota : Picture Window Books, a Capstone imprint, [2018] | Series: Leaders doing headstands |
Audience: Ages 6–12. | Audience: Grades K to 3. | Includes bibliographical references and index.
Identifiers: LCCN 2017008204 | ISBN 9781515815754 (library binding) | ISBN 9781515815792 (paperback) | ISBN 9781515815839 (eBook PDF)
Subjects: LCSH: Armstrong, Neil, 1930–2012—Juvenile literature. | Astronauts—United States—Biography—Juvenile literature. | Project Apollo (U.S.)—
History—Juvenile literature. | Space flight to the moon—History—Juvenile literature.
Classification: LCC TL789.85.A75 W43 2018 | DDC 629.450092 [B]—dc23
LC record available at https://lccn.loc.gov/2017008204

Printed and bound in the United States of America.
052018   000498